mini saga
competition 2007
for Primary Schools from Young Writers in association with

Tiny Tales

West Midlands

First published in Great Britain in 2007 by
Young Writers, Remus House, Coltsfoot Drive,
Peterborough, PE2 9JX
Tel (01733) 890066 Fax (01733) 313524
All Rights Reserved

© Copyright Contributors 2007
SB ISBN 978-1-84431-315-0

Disclaimer
Young Writers has maintained every effort
to publish stories that will not cause offence.
Any stories, events or activities relating to individuals
should be read as fictional pieces and not construed
as real-life character portrayal.

Foreword

Young Writers was established in 1991, with the aim of encouraging the children and young adults of today to think and write creatively. Our latest primary school competition, *Tiny Tales*, posed an exciting challenge for these young authors: to write, in no more than fifty words, a story encompassing a beginning, a middle and an end. We call this the mini saga.

Tiny Tales West Midlands is our latest offering from the wealth of young talent that has mastered this incredibly challenging form. With such an abundance of imagination, humour and ability evident in such a wide variety of stories, these young writers cannot fail to enthral and excite with every tale.

Contents

Bentley Drive Primary School, Walsall
Mehvish Amjid (11) 13
Abdul Aslam (10) 14
Jayesh Gumber (11) 15
Jessica Fizer (11) 16
Lewis Hill (11) 17

Collingbourne Primary School, Collingbourne
Callum Hollis (10) 18
Jack Saunders (10) 19
Connor Corkhill (9) 20
Azia Tobin (11) 21
Macauley Broscombe (10) 22
Katie Stevens (11) 23
Andrew Macdonald (10) 24
Megan Richardson (11) 25
Levi Morphy (11) 26
Sophie Mowle (9) 27
Jordan Pagett (10) 28
Aimee Hewitt (11) 29
Summer Gale (9) 30
Dayna Hiscock (11) 31
Conor Kennedy (11) 32
Katie Taylor (9) 33

Dickens Heath Community Primary School, Dickens Heath
Daniel Finnerty (8) 34
Molly Dawson (8) 35
Ellena Fennell (8) 36
Joshua Middlemiss (8) 37

Eversfield Preparatory School, Solihull
James Stansfield (10) 38
Sophie Hill (10) 39
Keelan Fadden-Hopper (11) 40
Ketan Chavda (10) 41

Fairhaven Primary School, Wordsley
Emily Brookes (10) 42
Rhianna Truman (10) 43
Emma Roberts (10) 44
Joseph Abbott (10) 45
Isabel Woodall (10) 46

George Fentham Endowed Primary School, Solihull
Robert Bromley (11) 47
Anna Claringbull (11) 48
Kathryn Jones (11) 49
Matthew Paveley (11) 50

Emma Collis (11) 51
Owen Lam (10) 52
Laura Wills (10) 53
Samuel Hiskett (10) 54
Joseph Byrne (10) 55
Cavan Painter (10) 56
Connie Ashton (10) 57
Gareth Lusty (10) 58
Alexander Davis (9) 59
Madeleine Burch (11) 60

Grangehurst Primary School, Coventry
Zhana Ivanova (11) 61
Elizabeth Holcroft (11) 62

Greenholm J&I School, Birmingham
Quanique Boyd (11) 63
Jordain Ballintine-Robinson (11) 64

Hasbury Primary School, Halesowen
Katherine Potter (8) 65
Peter Dear (9) 66
Ellie Layton (9) 67
Amy Lees (9) 68

Holy Rosary RC Primary School, Wolverhampton
Hugo Evans (10) 69
Siobhan MacDonald (10) 70
Joshua Baxter (10) 71
Salih Matsemela (10) 72

Holy Souls Catholic Primary School, Acocks Green
Áine M M Healy (10) 73

Kingshurst Junior School, Kingshurst
Robyn Moy (11) 74
Aleksandra Skrzypczak (11) 75
Elle Westwood (10) 76
Chelsey Steward (10) 77
Amy Johnson (11) 78
Zara Taylor (11) 79

Little Sutton Primary School, Sutton Coldfield
Danae David-Ferlance (11) 80
Jessica Walker (10) 81
Ella Sheasby (11) 82
Matthew Allsopp (11) 83
Danielle Gee (10) 84
Lee Richards (10) 85
Charlotte Bryant (11) 86
Georgina Louisa Higgs (10) 87
Jack Seifas (11) 88
Beth Henry (11) 89
Maya Mistry (11) 90
Ben Austin (10) 91
Katie Land (10) 92
Ella Follis (11) 93
George Burdock (11) 94
Daniel Blythe (11) 95
Charlotte Cooper (10) 96

Amrika Harrison (11) 97
Taylor Dunn (10) 98
Francesca Westwood (10) 99
Matthew Chancellor (10) 100
Rebecca Yardley (11) 101

Lutley Primary School, Halesowen
Molly Street (11) 102
Ellis Metcalf (11) 103
Katherine Hawthorne (11) 104
Matthew Chadd (11) 105
Jordan Smith (10) 106
Annie Pitman (10) 107
Jordan Aspbury (11) 108
Chloe Workman (11) 109
Christian Jones (10) 110
Imogen Mellor (11) 111
Rebecca Clarke (11) 112
Leah Paddock (11) 113
Kieran Powell (11) 114
Kate Davis (11) 115
Benjamin Cartwright (11) 116
Siân George (11) 117
Katie Billingham (11) 118
Amy Partridge (11) 119
Matthew North (11) 120
Jessica Sinclair (11) 121
Nicole Corbett (11) 122
Louise Rollings (10) 123
Sally Sinclair (11) 124
Charlotte Little (11) 125

Bethany Humphries (11) 126
George Ashby (11) 127
Pollyanna Sullivan (11) 128
Elinor Cole (11) 129
Lydia Ramsden (11) 130
Jacob Upcott (11) 131
Amy Ryan (11) 132
Lauren Embrey (11) 133

Mount Nod Primary School, Coventry
Thomas Sprogis (11) 134
Shannon Stevenson (11) 135
Connie Teggin (10) 136
Sarah Didcott (10) 137

St Bernadette's RC Primary School, Yardley
Jeneitha-Ashley Walker (10) 138
Laura Ryan (10) 139
Cathareen Babu (10) 140
Yanieke Neale Williams (10) 141
Molly Nevin (10) 142
Athif Hussain (9) 143
Daniel Tonks (10) 144
Josh Walsh (10) 145
Joseph Ball (9) 146
Brittany MacDonald (10) 147
Alexandra Spence (9) 148
Bethany Smallwood (10) 149
Adam Smiley (10) 150

Georgia McGuire (10) 151
Samantha Gartland (9) 152
Shannon Meakin (10) 153
Ashley Wear (10) 154
Aimee Rose (10) 155
Phillippa Hunter (10) 156
Abigail Hunter (10) 157
Aimé Dickson (10) 158

St Catherine of Siena RC Primary School, Lee Bank
Jamilah Mohammed (9) 159
Sineade Bates (10) 160

St Joseph's Catholic Primary School, Darlaston
Natalie Maybury (11) 161

St Mary's RC Primary School, Wednesbury
Abigail Armstrong (10) 162
Paige Bullock (10) 163
Paige Callear (11) 164
Nicole Caulfield (11) 165
Rachel Cutler (11) 166
Aliya De Vini (11) 167
Chantelle Grove (11) 168
Ryan Flowers (11) 169
Megan McNally (11) 170
Siobhan Wilkes (11) 171
Tomasz Zielinski (11) 172

St Patrick's RC Primary School, Walsall
Katie Ellis (11) 173
Denise Pacurza (11) 174
Charlotte Rich (10) 175
Georgia Allen (10) 176
Joseph McNally (10) 177
Emily Mace (10) 178
Callum Wigley (10) 179
Michaela Jenkins (10) 180
Sophie Dabbs (10) 181
Melissa Powell (10) 182
Harry Smith (10) 183
Caoimhe Harvey (10) 184
Lucy Westwood (9) 185
Bonnie Ryder (11) 186
Shannondeep Gill (11) 187
Amber Wilson (10) 188
Leah Anslow (11) 189
Ryan Edge (10) 190
Lauren Aulton (10) 191
Simran Singh Uppal (11) 192
Sian Gallagher (11) 193
Zoë Langley (11) 194
Clare Newton Sheppard (11) 195
Antoinette Chiwambo (11) 196

Shirestone CP School, Tile Cross
Thomas Gilfoyle (10) 197
Kimberley Parrish (11) 198
Tori Lynch (11) 199

Hayley Bickley (11)	200
Jessica Aldridge (11)	201
Kimberly Wedderburn (10)	202
Lamariya Alexander (10)	203
Niall Rowe (11)	204
Nicole Yates (11)	205
Nicole Bell (10)	206
Kieran Moogan (10)	207
Guy Brayne (10)	208
Kirsty Prescott (10)	209
Nathan Davies (10)	210
Corey Hodges (10)	211
Emily Williams (8)	212
Georgia Mahon (8)	213
Shannon Rainey (8)	214
Chloe Short (8)	215
George Facer (8)	216
Reece Drakeley (9)	217
Chad Fennell (11)	218
Connor Bryan (11)	219
Kelly Brayne (11)	220

The Ridge Primary School, Wollaston

Zoe Fincher (11)	221
Jenny Supple (11)	222
Jay Hill (10)	223
Edmund Roffe (11)	224
Thomas Mander (11)	225
Samuel Price (11)	226
James Pennington (11)	227
Joe Upton (11)	228
Lauren Simmonds (11)	229
Daniella Beach (11)	230
Lisa-Marie Powell (11)	231
Kirsty Trevis (11)	232
Emma Griffiths (11)	233
Bethany Howell (11)	234
Josh Hill (10)	235
Jacob Humphries (11)	236
Chelsea Heathcote (10)	237
Jake Shilvock (11)	238
Amy Checketts (11)	239
Jasdeep Kang (10)	240
Alicia Hewins (11)	241

Walmley Junior School, Walmley

Leah Rudd (9)	242
Beth Crawford (9)	243
Jack Richards (8)	244
Mandip Jhitta (8)	245
Amelia Bow (8)	246
Charlie Hale (8)	247
Samuel Jones (9)	248
Georgia Fielding (9)	249
Lindsay Ewer (7)	250
Kayleigh Sheward (9)	251
Charlie Fellows (7)	252
Phoebe McHale (8)	253
Scarlett Byfield-Levell (10)	254
Joe Willetts (8)	255
Vincent Peters (8)	256
Tommy Roberts (7)	257

Grace Chaundy (8) 258
Mathew Williams (8) 259
Alex Nevin (8) 260
Alex Reely (8) 261
Olivia Austin (7) 262
Hannah Peters (8) 263
Sophie Haynes (8) 264
Kyra Nagra (8) 265
Matthew Calvin (8) 266
Ashley Ward (8) 267
Natasha Davis (8) 268
Rebecca Turner (7) 269
Oliver Perrins (9) 270
Lauren Harris (9) 271
George Evans (9) 272
Michael Hartigan (9) 273
Remmi Kennedy (9) 274
Hannah Walker (9) 275
Catherine Read (10) 276
Claire Matthews (9) 277
Lauren Cox (9) 278
Nickie Morris (8) 279
Priya Sandhu (9) 280
Georgia Archer (9) 281
David Fentham (9) 282
Kellie Brooke (9) 283

Yew Tree Primary School, Walsall
Arun Kalwan (11) 284
Dale Groves (11) 285
David Robinson (10) 286
Tamjid Ahmed (10) 287
Ashley Durnall (11) 288
Ryan Hollingworth (11) 289
Jordan Spittle (11) 290
Gabriella Orthodoxou (11) 291
Danny Hill (11) 292
Calum Richardson (11) 293
Emma Carter (11) 294
Aleisha Lawley (11) 295
Callum Whitehouse (11) 296

The Mini Sagas

The Witch

Walking in the street on a cloudy day I was grabbed. I knew it was a witch because of the clothing. She took me to her lair and got a potion and dropped me in a bowl of hot water!

Mehvish Amjid (11)
Bentley Drive Primary School, Walsall

SATs

'Ah, at last SATs are over, now we can relax,' said Michael, putting his pencil in the pot. Suddenly another sheet fell onto Michael's table.
'Yeah, SATs are over but not for you they ain't,' said Mrs Jenkins.
'Damn my hands are aching!'

Abdul Aslam (10)
Bentley Drive Primary School, Walsall

The Terror Of The Eagle

Slowly the eagle swooped down looking for prey. Me, in this case! Quickly I jumped into a nearby cave. It was pitch-black dark. Suddenly, I heard a sound getting closer. *What should I do?* I thought to myself. Oh no! I had fallen deeper into the cave …

Jayesh Gumber (11)
Bentley Drive Primary School, Walsall

The Fairies

Waking up I remembered the fairies. Excited, I got dressed and ran downstairs, opened the back door and ran out. Awkwardly, I walked round the pond to the back of the garden. Sitting on the damp green grass I started to sing the fairy song. Suddenly they appeared.

Jessica Fizer (11)
Bentley Drive Primary School, Walsall

The Meteor Army

Hurtling through space, several meteors targeted a lone planet for collision. Awkwardly it teetered on the edge of the universe, prone to falling off. In the meteor's interior a vast array of aliens chanted: 'We shall dominate this planet Earth!' Excitedly they prepared for the annihilation of the Emperor planet.

Lewis Hill (11)
Bentley Drive Primary School, Walsall

Haunted House

Callum and Sasha found a haunted house. They said, 'Let's check it out.' They opened the door slowly, they found a zombie. The zombie chased them down the stairs, but the door was locked! They found an open window, jumped out to find it had been a big joke! Ha!

Callum Hollis (10)
Collingbourne Primary School, Collingbourne

Flames

Long, long ago, there was little dragon called Flames. Flames lived in a cave near the beach. Every day Flames would come out of his cave to search for food. But one morning Flames wasn't there. Everyone was looking everywhere and finally they found him in the sea.

Jack Saunders (10)
Collingbourne Primary School, Collingbourne

Untitled

A boy was kicking his football, *kick, kick,* higher and higher. Suddenly it bounced next door. Out came a scary old lady. He had got caught out! 'Connor what did I tell you?' then she disappeared. He waited, crept closer, grabbed the ball. He got away this time! Ha!

Connor Corkhill (9)
Collingbourne Primary School, Collingbourne

The Pearly Gates

I must be crazy, I could feel myself rising slowly into the clouds. I tried to scream but I couldn't. I saw the shimmering pearly gates glowing fabulously. No, this was not real! I saw Mum trapped inside. I was falling now, I was lying on a hospital bed, alone.

Azia Tobin (11)
Collingbourne Primary School, Collingbourne

The Sloth

The sloth slept lazily on the branch, surrounded by a blanket of leaves. Then the tree branch started to creak loudly, causing the sloth to awaken.
He was very scared as he watched the shadow tiptoe across the branch.
'Wake up,' yelled the mother sloth. It was Mum.

Macauley Broscombe (10)
Collingbourne Primary School, Collingbourne

The Dracula Dream

Bill was eating his tea. He was so tired after football practice he fell asleep in his dinner. Bill dreamed of the new film 'Dracula Mansion'. Dracula loomed out of the shadows. He's here! A pair of fangs met his gaze.
'Bill, wake up,' cried Mum. Ketchup smothered his face.

Katie Stevens (11)
Collingbourne Primary School, Collingbourne

Superman Saves Sam

'Joe to you.'
'OK, I'll score a goal.' He tried scoring a goal but kicked it wrong, it went through the old lady's window. As Sam was climbing out, the woman caught his leg and tied him to a chair. Suddenly Superman flew through the window and saved Sam.

Andrew Macdonald (10)
Collingbourne Primary School, Collingbourne

The Ravens Of Night

They were coming, the ravens, killers of baby sparrows, like Floss. Night was coming. They came with the night. Suddenly Floss heard the sound of wings behind her. The ravens would get her. Strong claws gripped Floss. She realised it wasn't raven's claws. Floss' mum had come to save her.

Megan Richardson (11)
Collingbourne Primary School, Collingbourne

Cosmo's Adventure

Cosmo was out in the snow when he saw … what was that? Argh! A Dog! Cosmo scrambled across the snow. 'Help! Help!' he miaowed. It was coming closer.
'Cosmo, stop, it's me.'
Cosmo stopped, the dog was - Mum!
'Oh Mum.' Cosmo bounded towards her.
'Come on, let's go home Cosmo!'

Levi Morphy (11)
Collingbourne Primary School, Collingbourne

Disaster Spell

In the tower, 10-year-old Sally stands alone with only a spell book, wand and cat for company. For fifteen long years Sally studies out of the ancient spell book and finds a spell: Zinglingting.
'Sally, why are you waving a pencil in your hand?' snapped Mrs Spell angrily!

Sophie Mowle (9)
Collingbourne Primary School, Collingbourne

An Alien Visiting Earth

One dark night a little boy called John saw a flying saucer. He put his coat and shoes on and went to the woods.

He saw the aliens coming out of the flying saucer. They looked around and went back inside the saucer and flew away amongst the bright stars.

Jordan Pagett (10)
Collingbourne Primary School, Collingbourne

The Jellyfish

Something hit me like lightning on my leg and back. I tried to turn around, my body was motionless and was numb. Opening my eyes I looked to the surface, there was a pulsing object above me. A jellyfish!
I opened my eyes - I saw my mum, she'd rescued me!

Aimee Hewitt (11)
Collingbourne Primary School, Collingbourne

The Three Bunnies

One day there was a girl called Debbie, she had three rabbits named Nugget, Horris and Jasper.

In a high field one day, Nugget ran away. Debbie was very upset. The snow came, the rabbit was still lost but then suddenly, Debbie turned and saw her bunny was back. Hooray!

Summer Gale (9)
Collingbourne Primary School, Collingbourne

The Scale And Fang

They're coming. Hunting me down like a deer. The Gorgons are hungry. I'm next. I just know it. 'Argh,' they've got me! They're pulling me, shaking me. Here come their fangs, glinting, gnarled teeth. I feel their breath …
'Jay,' cries Mum, 'get out of bed! You are late for school!'

Dayna Hiscock (11)
Collingbourne Primary School, Collingbourne

The Dream

Michael kicked his football down a chimney. He found a collapsed wall and walked in. He heard strange noises. As he walked through he fell down a hole onto a table. An old lady strapped him down and ate him. His mum called him for breakfast, but what a shock …

Conor Kennedy (11)
Collingbourne Primary School, Collingbourne

Scary Dream

I'm alone … where am I?
I'm lost in the middle of a dark, spooky forest.
I hear creepy footsteps getting closer. I'm
scared, my heart is beating like a drum - I run.
What's that strange noise? Oh, it's my
alarm clock. I'm safe in my cosy bed - I was
dreaming.

Katie Taylor (9)
Collingbourne Primary School, Collingbourne

Spooky Museum

It stood before him, towering over him, jaws wide open. Hideous eyes staring at Leo, he hoped it wasn't lunchtime. He trembled as he thought it was about to pounce. Leo thought it was moving closer.

Suddenly, 'There are other things in this museum than that stegosaurus,' said Mommy firmly.

Daniel Finnerty (8)
Dickens Heath Community Primary School, Dickens Heath

Camping

Crunch, creak, zip. Argh! Annie thought, *was it a fox? I know, quick, hide in your sleeping bag. Head in, bottom down. Breathe quietly, you'll be fine. Oh no! He's seen me - stay as you are then he'll forget. Go on you can do it Annie.*
'Tea anyone?' said Dad.

Molly Dawson (8)
Dickens Heath Community Primary School, Dickens Heath

The Ghost Trick

One night when James was in bed he saw a ghost in his room. He was terrified and he felt like pulling his hair out. It was that scary. His mother called him for a drink or something like that. It was his little sister pretending to be the ghost.

Ellena Fennell (8)
Dickens Heath Community Primary School, Dickens Heath

The Story Of HMS Nimble

This was the final battle. This decided who won the war. This was it.
Suddenly the guns opened fire … *Boom!* One of the guns blew up. *Boom!* The ship's bridge blew up. *Glug!* The battleship sank.
'Time to get out of the bath now,' said Mum.
'Ohhh Muuum!' moaned Josh.

Joshua Middlemiss (8)
Dickens Heath Community Primary School, Dickens Heath

Untitled

I crawled to cover, blood dripping from my gaping wounds. Gun in hands, I was ready to go back into the terrifying battlefield. I stood, a giant lump entered my throat. I ran back into the nightmare of war.

'James, it's lunchtime, time to put down your action figures.'

James Stansfield (10)
Eversfield Preparatory School, Solihull

The Mummy

I was in bed, someone came upstairs to bed. Something crept into my room. I tried to scream but nothing came out. *A monster*, I thought to myself. I tried to wake up, but it was real - I wasn't dreaming. The light turned on, I sat up and saw … Mummy!

Sophie Hill (10)
Eversfield Preparatory School, Solihull

The Experiment That Went Wrong

I stood beside Sir's desk, watching the experiment. Suddenly an orange beast leapt out of the darkness. Its long claws stretched out towards us. We knew success would draw black blood. I jumped back in fear. Sir reached over and turned the gas tap off. The beast was gone forever.

Keelan Fadden-Hopper (11)
Eversfield Preparatory School, Solihull

The Monster

I crept into the abandoned house, a floorboard creaked, except I wasn't moving! So I followed the noise but there was more than one noise. Then suddenly a vampire popped out, then a mummy. I screamed and ran for my life. Then came a werewolf which said, 'Happy Hallowe'en!'

Ketan Chavda (10)
Eversfield Preparatory School, Solihull

The Race

Bang! went the gun as I crossed the starting line. Instantly my tummy flipped over as I took the lead. The sound of footsteps came closer, but I didn't dare look back. The roaring of the crowd got louder as I crossed the finishing line. I had won!

Emily Brookes (10)
Fairhaven Primary School, Wordsley

There Goes The World

Lions, monkeys, elephants, leopards, cheetahs and tigers, they are everywhere! More lions, more monkeys, more elephants, more cheetahs and more tigers. The world is getting full, too full! More and more animals appear. Then more of you, twins, triplets, even quads of you! Then a great big *bang! Oh no!*

Rhianna Truman (10)
Fairhaven Primary School, Wordsley

Petrified

'Bedtime,' shouted Mum. 'Remember the upstairs light isn't working.'
My heart jumped into my throat. I hated the dark. Looking up I saw a ghostly figure. As I climbed, trembling, something brushed against my leg. Cautiously reaching down I realised it wasn't a ghost, it was my cat Millie!

Emma Roberts (10)
Fairhaven Primary School, Wordsley

A Terrifying Experience

I walked into the whitewashed building feeling very afraid. I was taken to a room with a leather seat, then green-gloved hands probed my mouth and then I felt a pain in my mouth vanish.
Later I got a brave child sticker and forgot my fear of the dentist.

Joseph Abbott (10)
Fairhaven Primary School, Wordsley

Unicorns

My body was shaking as I got onto the unicorn's back. My stomach started to hurt and we began to go up. *Argh!*
Back on the ground I felt more worried than I was in the air. I can't believe that I have a big fear of travelling on unicorns!

Isabel Woodall (10)
Fairhaven Primary School, Wordsley

The Aussie Surfer

It's midday in Australia and Rob Zino was teaching some children how to surf. He'd said that he'd got a new surfboard the day before. Rob had caught a large wave. Suddenly a shark lunged from below the water and took Rob under. Rob's board came back without him

...

Robert Bromley (11)
George Fentham Endowed Primary School, Solihull

The Weird Sound

I tiptoed downstairs, my heart pounding. I clutched my teddy and slowly opened the kitchen door. What was that sound? I crept into the garage hearing even louder bangs. What was it? I looked around and saw my trainers thumping in the washing machine. So that's what woke me up!

Anna Claringbull (11)
George Fentham Endowed Primary School, Solihull

The Mysterious Attic

Her feet controlled her as she shuffled up the attic staircase. She peeped in cautiously, not knowing what to expect. She stepped in, *bang!* The door slammed shut. The light was no more. Trapped. Suddenly a hand gripped her shoulder, she froze. A shadow sprinted away. She glanced round … nothing!

Kathryn Jones (11)
George Fentham Endowed Primary School, Solihull

Scare

Drip, drip, drip. The water around us was rising with nothing to stop it from coming under the tent door. There was no one to hear our cries. Suddenly I heard a bang, Tom dropped to the floor. Another bang and the last thing I heard was my mobile ringing.

Matthew Paveley (11)
George Fentham Endowed Primary School, Solihull

Home Alone

She was on her own for the first time. Her clammy fingers fumbled for the light switch. The light flickered and died on her. Suddenly she heard a noise - a burglar? She crept downstairs as the front door flung open. It was horrible, it was her terrifying older brother!

Emma Collis (11)
George Fentham Endowed Primary School, Solihull

Captured

He crept along the window and tiptoed left to right. He was on a mission to capture the Queen's crown. But Phillip heard some footsteps and suddenly the police turned up. Phillip was caught already, before he even had the chance to look at the Queen's beautiful crown.

Owen Lam (10)
George Fentham Endowed Primary School, Solihull

Kidnapped

It was night. Daisy was alone, walking through the woods. She was going home from her friend's house. Suddenly from nowhere jumped a man, wearing a black mask! He tied up Daisy and pulled her through the trees. He told her that from now on she would be his servant.

Laura Wills (10)
George Fentham Endowed Primary School, Solihull

The Dream

As night fell the first shot sounded. Suddenly the houses were ablaze. The war had started. Vehicles raced around, men dropped to the ground and bombs fell like rain. Then a familiar voice called out, 'Sam, wake up, we don't want to be late for school again, do we now?'

Samuel Hiskett (10)
George Fentham Endowed Primary School, Solihull

The Midnight Frog

It was a cold and dark night. I could hear the rain dropping on the roof. I could hear a noise coming from under my bed. I looked under. There was a little green frog. 'Phew,' I sighed. The next day I put it out so it could run free.

Joseph Byrne (10)
George Fentham Endowed Primary School, Solihull

The Beast

As the beast rose from his hole I ran as fast as I could. Home seemed like it was miles away. When I was home and indoors the beast was bashing down the door, so we ran to the kitchen.
As the beast came in, he grabbed me, but …

Cavan Painter (10)
George Fentham Endowed Primary School, Solihull

What A Night!

It was Hallowe'en. The streets were pitch-black. I heard a strange cackle in the distance. 'A witch,' I screamed. The old lady ran towards me screeching with laughter. Suddenly the street lights flashed back on. 'Oh Gran!' I groaned, 'that pointy black hat just doesn't suit you!'

Connie Ashton (10)
George Fentham Endowed Primary School, Solihull

The Red Message

A mysterious blob appeared on my maths book just after break. It was a rusty-red colour. Maybe it's a message from a ghost ... Another blob appeared two minutes later. Who was sending me these messages?

Mrs Corfield walked past. 'Gareth, do you know you have a nose bleed?'

Gareth Lusty (10)
George Fentham Endowed Primary School, Solihull

The Experiment

The professor turned on the power. There was a flash of light and the creature on the table lifted its head and gradually rose, as if awakening from sleep.
If you'd listened that night you'd have heard strangling noises as the creature attacked. Slowly it disappeared into the night …

Alexander Davis (9)
George Fentham Endowed Primary School, Solihull

The Face At The Window

As she approached the rain-drenched window, a pale face appeared as a bolt of lightning struck the tall spire silhouetted against the pale night sky. She screamed, a blood-curdling scream, which echoed all over the deserted church. Suddenly a pale bony hand shoved her towards the window … *Smash!*

Madeleine Burch (11)
George Fentham Endowed Primary School, Solihull

The Secret

Running as fast as their feet could carry them. The children were so scared they felt their throats closing up and sweat was dripping off them. They stopped and in front of them was …

Zhana Ivanova (11)
Grangehurst Primary School, Coventry

The Incredible Medicine

Grandma and Charlie were in the kitchen making a medicine. They added everything they could find. When Grandma went to try it she grew fat then Charlie tried some, he grew a beard. The place was a mess and Mum was coming back from the doctors. She came in screaming.

Elizabeth Holcroft (11)
Grangehurst Primary School, Coventry

Trapped In School

Excitedly, I collected my bag from school. My friend Emma was waiting in the car. Yes - got it. *Bang!* Oh no, someone closed the door. I was locked in the dark school. 'Help!' *Creak!* Miss Adams opened the door, 'You coming out now?'
'Yes.' *Phew!* I'm out!

Quanique Boyd (11)
Greenholm J&I School, Birmingham

The Three Blind Mice

The three blind mice were playing with a dice,
when Mrs Macice came in and said, 'I hope you are playing nice.'
'Of course,' they all said, 'but we are very hungry and we are in need of some rice.'
'Of course you are, it's very nice.'
Yum, yum!

Jordain Ballintine-Robinson (11)
Greenholm J&I School, Birmingham

The Skateboard That Did Stunts By Itself

The skateboard was Daniel's, who lived on Instone Road. It came to life while he was walking in the park. He did not notice it was remote controlled. A boy called Peter had put it on.
'Argh,' Daniel yelled. Peter showed him the remote.
'I'll get you,' Daniel yelled.

Katherine Potter (8)
Hasbury Primary School, Halesowen

The Killer Book

'I've lost my book!' sobbed Jack. 'Where could it be? ... At last I've found it.'
Jack was eight years old with brown eyes and blond hair. He'd found his book which he had never opened. Jack opened his book. Suddenly it shot out a poison dart. Jack was in Heaven.

Peter Dear (9)
Hasbury Primary School, Halesowen

The Genuine Jewel

Rover barked furiously as they dug at the ground. Holly looked down to find a bright red jewel. Cloe said it was her birthday. Holly gave her the jewel. She now had magical powers. Holly was really jealous.
They aren't friends now but what happens in the future is another story.

Ellie Layton (9)
Hasbury Primary School, Halesowen

Swimming

Enjoying swimming, I was alerted by a scream.
A drowning baby! Her sister was scared, crying,
shocked. I swam to the baby, swam underneath
the water. I just caught the baby, grabbed her
and gave it back to her older sister.
I can't believe it, I saved a baby's life!

Amy Lees (9)
Hasbury Primary School, Halesowen

The Last Dragon

A long time ago, in a mystical forest, lived an almighty dragon. One day he didn't have a friend, he was all alone, then he saw another dragon. He flew over and asked if she would be his friend and she said, 'Yes, I will be your best friend forever.'

Hugo Evans (10)
Holy Rosary RC Primary School, Wolverhampton

A Night In The Forest

One dark night, in a place called Smallville, a girl called Sharn was going into a woodland. The girls in her class said it was a sleepover, but when she looked for them they weren't there. Her mom started to look for her, she wasn't there. She wasn't seen again.

Siobhan MacDonald (10)
Holy Rosary RC Primary School, Wolverhampton

The Power Of Noise

The corridors were empty. The classrooms were silent except for the kindergarten class. Things were being tossed from the door as Hank trotted through the hallways. His heels broke the silence. He finally reached the class. The class was roaring and ear-splitting. After 6 weeks the children were reformed.

Joshua Baxter (10)
Holy Rosary RC Primary School, Wolverhampton

Ant Lost

Once there was an ant, it got lost by falling off a cliff. Nobody found it for days.
After one year it was found in a cave. They took the ant to its parents. They were very pleased to see their little ant again. They had a huge party.

Salih Matsemela (10)
Holy Rosary RC Primary School, Wolverhampton

Almost Atlantis

The brook's banks burst - water gushed rapidly towards us. I stared helplessly as Daddy waded across the road. Mightily he fought off the attacking debris and fearlessly bailed gallons of murky water from the danger zone. Breathless I watched the vortex disappear down the dark drain. The flood was over.

Áine M M Healy (10)
Holy Souls Catholic Primary School, Acocks Green

Untitled

I've paid my £5, it's my turn next. I'm moving up a robotic leg. Looking down everybody looks like ants! I'm trembling with excitement, 'Argh!' I'm falling. It feels so alone in the air. *Whoo*, I'm shot back up! My feet firmly on the ground! That was a brilliant bungee.

Robyn Moy (11)
Kingshurst Junior School, Kingshurst

The Victorian Times

We were in the small village, which didn't look very modern. This village looked very, very old, just like a Victorian village. People looked like Victorian people too. We've moved back to the Victorian times! 'Help!' I was shouting. Then I saw a board, *'Welcome to the Victorian open air museum'*.

Aleksandra Skrzypczak (11)
Kingshurst Junior School, Kingshurst

Tracy Beaker

I am full of attitude and have curly hair. I have been dumped back at the dumping ground 3 times. I am sick of the dumping ground. I hate Justine Littlewood.
One day the electricity went out and Jackey was scared and I was lying on her bed cuddling her.

Elle Westwood (10)
Kingshurst Junior School, Kingshurst

Ghost Attack

It was the year 1999. Something was banging its way up the staircase. 'Argh!' I screamed as my door opened and nobody was there. I cried for my mum and dad, they didn't come. I felt I was alone. It came closer and closer. It grabbed me. I screamed and …

Chelsey Steward (10)
Kingshurst Junior School, Kingshurst

The Scary Thing

I was sitting down on the sofa and I heard a noise. It sounded like a crunching sound. It smelt like my favourite cereal, Cheerios. I got up quickly, I followed the sound. It was coming from behind the furniture. I looked around the corner, it was a puppy. Cute!

Amy Johnson (11)
Kingshurst Junior School, Kingshurst

Sister Attack

I was there, right in the middle. It jumped at me. I started to attack back, but it was no good. Then it was all over. My beautiful painted nails were chipped. I wish I had not stolen my sister's teddy bear now!

Zara Taylor (11)
Kingshurst Junior School, Kingshurst

Where Was I?

As I entered the freaky castle a shiver travelled down my spine. My heartbeat grew faster every second. What was to become of me? Was I being watched? I pushed a door that looked old and rusty. It creaked loudly. There was a table full of marvellous food.

Danae David-Ferlance (11)
Little Sutton Primary School, Sutton Coldfield

No Way Out

The thunder roared, the lightning struck. It was going round in circles. *Oh no, I'm in a mirror maze,* I thought to myself, *there's no way out! I'm stuck.* 'Help'. My heart started to pound. The clouds burst open, rain poured out. I frantically ran … 'Help, there's no way out!'

Jessica Walker (10)
Little Sutton Primary School, Sutton Coldfield

The Tower

Roaring thunder and lightning boomed as I walked - afraid - towards the terrifying tower waiting for me. My heart was beating faster with every step I took; while the howling wind whistled, or was it the haunted tower calling me? Then an icy hand grabbed my shoulder. I screamed and ran …

Ella Sheasby (11)
Little Sutton Primary School, Sutton Coldfield

Beasts From Another World

I was sitting on a rock. Then a huge beast appeared from nowhere and began ravenously chewing my rucksack. Suddenly another beast rose from a huge hole in the ground. Before I knew it, I was surrounded by beasts.
'What a great story, Alex,' said Mom.
'I agree,' whimpered Dad.

Matthew Allsopp (11)
Little Sutton Primary School, Sutton Coldfield

A Sweet Sensation

I sank into the powdery sherbet. I could smell the candyfloss floating in the sky. I walked through the crumbly powder as I drank icing out of a buttercup. Suddenly something caught my eye. It was raining pear drops. I bent down to touch my luxurious sweet …
'School time, Danielle!'

Danielle Gee (10)
Little Sutton Primary School, Sutton Coldfield

Tiny Tales West Midlands

Alien Kidnap

I knew it was an alien. I could tell by its eyes. They were red. It was just about to gobble me up, but there was one thing, I didn't want to die. So I had to think of a plan, and that was how to kill it really silently.

Lee Richards (10)
Little Sutton Primary School, Sutton Coldfield

Mental Sight

It was black as night, the gate shuddered on its rusty, creaking hinges. Rain drummed on my pounding head; suddenly, I heard a voice. Who was there? Someone put their hand on my shoulder. 'It's time to go back to the mental hospital,' explained the nurse.
'Nooo!' I screamed.

Charlotte Bryant (11)
Little Sutton Primary School, Sutton Coldfield

Silence Comes ...

It was on that night, the very night he came. The night turned wild ... the stranger made their way up the path as the lightning tore at the black sky with fury in its presence. I caught a glimpse of his bleak face. He would kill me. Silence suddenly came.

Georgina Louisa Higgs (10)
Little Sutton Primary School, Sutton Coldfield

The Thing

Boom, the door came down. I saw a big, dark, scary shadow. *Zap! Zap!* The thing shot at me. I ran. The thing was close behind, then suddenly I fell! *'Argh!'* I screamed in pain. I looked up and saw it. It looked at me, I screamed loudly in fright.

Jack Seifas (11)
Little Sutton Primary School, Sutton Coldfield

The Castle

Cautiously I strutted toward the ominous castle. Indigo trailed behind me shaking. A flash of lightning flicked, making a nearby graveyard very visible indeed. 'Indigo,' I bellowed, frantically spinning round. She was nowhere to be seen … where could she be? I headed for the graveyard! Suddenly a hand grabbed me …

Beth Henry (11)
Little Sutton Primary School, Sutton Coldfield

The Death-Defying Experience

My heart started beating, my legs started to wobble. I was all alone in the big, mysterious castle. Rain spattered down on the window, like a rattlesnake. The misty air lingered on as I crept forward. A shiver ran down my spine. I was all alone. *Crash! Bang!*

Maya Mistry (11)
Little Sutton Primary School, Sutton Coldfield

Noises!

There was a bang at the door. Cautiously someone crept to the door. He was petrified. *Bang! Bang!* He flung open the door in fright; there was … nothing! There were still noises; this time, *crash!*

He opened his eyes. He was staring at the mystery mansion …

Ben Austin (10)
Little Sutton Primary School, Sutton Coldfield

Untitled

Crack! The rusty old gate opened. There before me was a ghost, floating around. What was I to do? My heart was beating faster and faster! As I ran away the ghost followed me! Was there a chance of getting away or was I done for?

Katie Land (10)
Little Sutton Primary School, Sutton Coldfield

The Haunted Coach

Stepping towards the towering coach, lightning flashed, whilst thunder beat like trembling elephants. I immediately saw a darting figure following me. The wind rustled through my long, wavy hair. My heart pounding, shivering with terror. I stumbled into the cold, rusty, old coach.
'What could it be … ?'

Ella Follis (11)
Little Sutton Primary School, Sutton Coldfield

Wonder Goal

Bang! 'What a goal,' screamed Ally McCoist. 'Top right corner, David Beckham, a brilliant free kick taker, sending England into the World Cup final.'

England were running around wild, everybody was on the pitch going mad. Suddenly two streakers ran onto the pitch. All of a sudden, police ran on …

George Burdock (11)
Little Sutton Primary School, Sutton Coldfield

A Face Of Mist

A shady figure tiptoed across the dark courtyard, his face covered by a black hood. He stopped, he was standing by an old gravestone, the wind whistled. *Bang!* The gravestone exploded. The figure flew backwards into a rattling gate, his hood fell back - but there was no face, just mist …

Daniel Blythe (11)
Little Sutton Primary School, Sutton Coldfield

Argh

Creak, the old gate of the haunted house opened. I walked through the rustling leaves. I pushed the door open. The rain beat on the windows. *Flash!* Lightning ripped through the sky. Thunder boomed across the fields behind the house. Footsteps got louder, my heart stopped. *Argh!*

Charlotte Cooper (10)
Little Sutton Primary School, Sutton Coldfield

Untitled

Creak! Cautiously Claire entered the forbidden worn out mansion, not knowing what to expect
…
Clash! 'Huh! He-hello, is anybody there?'
Whoosh! Claire felt somebody swiftly go past her. She turned her whole body round, but no one was there …

Amrika Harrison (11)
Little Sutton Primary School, Sutton Coldfield

The Haunting

Creak! The old, rusty gate slowly opened. I stumbled forwards cautiously, shivering with fright. Suddenly, stood in front of me was a tall black figure! The fierce thunder started roaring. I started stepping backwards rapidly, but the tall, black figure quickly chased after me! Was I ever going to escape … ?

Taylor Dunn (10)
Little Sutton Primary School, Sutton Coldfield

The Witch Ghost

A gloomy howl lingered over the factory. The witch ghost loomed over, watching for humans to feast on. There stood a small boy (a snack for the witch.) She sneered, fangs showing. *Crack,* she broke the boy's neck. The witch, small boy in hand, swept up to eat her snack!

Francesca Westwood (10)
Little Sutton Primary School, Sutton Coldfield

Ghost Of Terror

It was a blistering night, rain thumping down. My heart was screaming with terror. I stepped in the spooky old house. The door screeched. I took several steps forward, then *smash,* the door slammed shut. The house was very scary. *Whoosh,* a ghost drifted past me, I screamed in fright.

Matthew Chancellor (10)
Little Sutton Primary School, Sutton Coldfield

The Selfish Snow Monster

It was Christmas Day, there were children making snowmen, but they never knew about the snow monster that came out of the snow and ate children. He didn't like children playing with his snow, and if someone did, he would find out who it was and eat them all up!

Rebecca Yardley (11)
Little Sutton Primary School, Sutton Coldfield

The Alien's Attack

He was lying there, lifeless. The alarming aliens had drained every bit of him. Now they were coming for me. Suddenly the door flew open, however I was prepared. My laser gun had done me proud. They fell with a colossal bang to the ground.
They were lying there lifeless.

Molly Street (11)
Lutley Primary School, Halesowen

Bermuda Square Mystery

It was Jess' fault … Now, mysterious sounds could be heard; moaning, groaning, screeching, sighing. Suddenly, people began to emerge from the swamp slime. Jess had to put it right. The world depended on her. She rounded up the ominous zombie creatures. Silence … she'd done it! But would they believe her?

Ellis Metcalf (11)
Lutley Primary School, Halesowen

Servants Can Find True Love

'Charles, where is it?' Charles was the servant for his fat lazy brothers. He was carrying breakfast upstairs to the beasts. He suddenly stopped in his tracks, a beautiful young woman came trotting in on a white stallion.
'Be my prince?' she proposed politely.
Charles agreed; they lived happily forever.

Katherine Hawthorne (11)
Lutley Primary School, Halesowen

Spooky Place

Joe stepped inside. The door slammed behind him. As he was trying to pull the door open, (it was locked), the kitchen door creaked. However the door was closed, it opened. Joe ran for it, but when he got there it slammed again. 'I've got to get out of here!'

Matthew Chadd (11)
Lutley Primary School, Halesowen

Mr President

Luke's X-wing blew up. He was so close. The room was quiet. 'I'm coming Mr President,' shouted the next pilot. 'What's your operating number?'
'I'm sorry Mr President, that falcon stopped me.'
'You're clear kid, blow this joint.'
'This is for you Mr President. Die Vader, death star destroyed, check.'

Jordan Smith (10)
Lutley Primary School, Halesowen

The Journey To Space

The rocket got ready to launch into space. Family and friends watched timidly. Hot gas flew out and we were in the sky. I could see the moon with my telescope.
After five days we crashed at Jupiter. Things flew down to Earth. It was horrible. My name's Neil Armstrong.

Annie Pitman (10)
Lutley Primary School, Halesowen

Monday Morning

I woke up. I hated Mondays. I wished it was Friday. School was approaching slowly. For breakfast I ate some Scotch pancakes also drank orange juice. Then I set off for school. I remembered after school I was going to my best friend's house. Mondays aren't so bad.

Jordan Aspbury (11)
Lutley Primary School, Halesowen

A Frozen World

All of a sudden I fell onto a cold frosty ground. The windy breeze tickled my throat and the icy frost bounced thunderously off the ground. In the distance I could see a sleigh with an ice queen sitting on it. She asked if I would join her. Me, frozen.

Chloe Workman (11)
Lutley Primary School, Halesowen

Dead

I ran and I ran, as a beastly beast chased after me, his eight arms tossing slime balls at me. I barged though windows. Flash, the big bad wolf came towards me. He blew me into a wood. *Chomp, chomp* goes the wolf's teeth into my flesh. Dead.

Christian Jones (10)
Lutley Primary School, Halesowen

The Crown

'Charming, where's my crown?' said Cinderella. She was about to attend a ball, a ball with posh ladies in fancy dress and fancy men in suits. But she could not go without her crown. She was in panic mode. She really, really, really needed her pretty, shiny, gold-plated crown.

Imogen Mellor (11)
Lutley Primary School, Halesowen

The Robe Of Skulls

'The robe of skulls is just at the end of the tomb,' she cackled. So the malevolent sorceress Lady Lana dodged and dived, but it was hard in a black velvet dress. As soon as she touched the robe a boulder crushed her. The robe was seen no more!

Rebecca Clarke (11)
Lutley Primary School, Halesowen

The Ghost Ride

The vehicle started to move. Carly wasn't the slightest bit scared. They went into a long, dark tunnel. A ghost suddenly appeared out of nowhere. A creaking door slowly followed. She shut her eyes tight. She got off quickly. She was never going on a ghost ride ever again.

Leah Paddock (11)
Lutley Primary School, Halesowen

The Intergalatic Ghost

Jack froze. Quivering in fear, he peeked through the hedges that surrounded him. The creature that laid before him was a bloodthirsty heart-munching ogre. Jack was too petrified to move. The brute was gazing around suspiciously, like he felt someone in his path. Suddenly the creature glared at him …

Kieran Powell (11)
Lutley Primary School, Halesowen

The Porthole Pool

I took a sip of the cool water that rippled in the morning breeze. It warmed me through as it flowed swiftly through my body. It gave me the feeling I was being welcomed.
Welcomed into another world … I had landed. Curiously I looked around, the mythical scenery was unfamiliar.

Kate Davis (11)
Lutley Primary School, Halesowen

Fury of Volcanoes

For days now an ominous rumbling had been coming from the depths of the volcano. Now a billowing plume of smoke is rising from its crater. Scientists have ordered an immediate evacuation of the town, in case of an eruption. A week later, it was burnt to ashes.

Benjamin Cartwright (11)
Lutley Primary School, Halesowen

Unknown Gnome

It was awakening. The ghastly beast was creeping closer …. and closer …
'Tally ho, ol' chap!', the monster bellowed down my ear. I screamed (well, miaowed in this case). He jumped back, 'I'm not going to eat you, I'm only a gnome!'
I was disappointed, there's never any action round here!

Siân George (11)
Lutley Primary School, Halesowen

Unusual Or Understanding?

'Kira you're an elephant, not an angel,' shouted Kira's auntie.
Suddenly there was an enormous blast of smoke, as vibrant and luminous as the sun, immediately something unusual spurted from the young baby. Beautiful - white as snow, something outstanding was discovered. It stood out like a sore thumb. Wings appeared …

Katie Billingham (11)
Lutley Primary School, Halesowen

The Girl's Shadow Nightmare

She could start to see a shadow forming in the doorway. It wasn't a human's reflection. As the creature slowly appeared in the sunlight, Lucy could start to see the monster heading towards her. Slime dripping from every point of its body. Lucy trembled then froze in silence.

Amy Partridge (11)
Lutley Primary School, Halesowen

Forest Fighter And The Wood Wreckers

It was a normal day in the dense Amazon rainforest … until now …
Suddenly the sound of knives slashing at shrubs could be heard. Habitats were being destroyed. Look - it's Forest Fighter, saviour of the forest. He grabbed a net and captured the environment hating group.
Another day to Forest Fighter!

Matthew North (11)
Lutley Primary School, Halesowen

Moonshine's Glory

The thundering hooves of Moonshine, my beautiful, velvet-black horse, made the world shake. Although I could barely see her, Moonshine's heartbeat was clear inside me; she was OK. Finally, she was going to live. My heart roared with joy and pride, like a lion. They had saved her!

Jessica Sinclair (11)
Lutley Primary School, Halesowen

Unknown Search

A house, precariously balanced on top of an enormous cliff, above jagged rocks. As I carefully tiptoed in, I heard a peculiar noise. I raced upstairs in search of something unknown - even I didn't know what I was looking for. All I knew was that I wasn't alone …

Nicole Corbett (11)
Lutley Primary School, Halesowen

In The Dark

Tap … tap … tap …
'Argh.' Eerie sounds oozed out of each room and Sam couldn't see anything! It was dark. Glowing eyes glistened at him! He ran as fast as lightning! Would he ever go back in again? Little did he know someone or something was following him. What would happen?

Louise Rollings (10)
Lutley Primary School, Halesowen

The Great Relief

'I could be your girlfriend,' sang Laura. 'Shut up,' screamed her younger brother. An eerie, inhuman boom sounded downstairs … they both jumped. Laura raced to the door, then, silently crept to the foot of the stairs. She peered down into the almost blackness. *Phew, it was Mom. Back from the gym.*

Sally Sinclair (11)
Lutley Primary School, Halesowen

The Enormous …

Beneath the crooked cottage, which precariously hung on a high precipice, lay ominous creatures, unknown to man. Timmy discovered this instantly and to his surprise they discovered him. However, this didn't stop Timmy. He peered over the jagged edge to find to his astonishment, an enormous boat and a fisherman.

Charlotte Little (11)
Lutley Primary School, Halesowen

Monster Disaster

Suddenly, as fast as lightning, a mysterious, ominous creature appeared in front of my eyes! What could it be? I was petrified. I lay there, still. Slowly the half-human monster crept towards me …
Sarah called Mom, 'Mom, help, there's a monster in my room, come quick …'
It was gone!

Bethany Humphries (11)
Lutley Primary School, Halesowen

The Chewing Gum Kid

Chew, chew, chew, went the Chewing Gum Kid.
Chewing here, chewing there, he would chew everywhere!
One day his mum was extremely annoyed and because she knew where he kept his *Trident Soft,* Tropical, *Trident Splash* - vanilla and mint, strawberry and lime, she took them away.
Ha! No more chewing!

George Ashby (11)
Lutley Primary School, Halesowen

I Don't Need A Prince

So, I'm Rapunzel, on my own, up in a tower, high in the sky. Bored to the bone. They explained a handsome prince would save me. Ten years later … still nothing. I was told to keep tidy, well, I'll rescue myself! Cut my hair, abseil down - and I needed *no prince!*

Pollyanna Sullivan (11)
Lutley Primary School, Halesowen

The Fire Beast

Was the world trembling or is it just me? thought Tom. He was encapsulated in a labyrinth, hiding from the fire beast.
He ran. *Thump, thump,* was that his heart racing or the mighty claws seeking him? Oops, he didn't mean to end up at a dead end.
Suddenly - blackness …

Elinor Cole (11)
Lutley Primary School, Halesowen

Hallowe'en Horror

It was just a normal day, which was going so well. Turned out to be very weird … There was a knock at the door. I opened it to see this unusual creature. 'Hello,' I said, puzzled. 'Happy Hallowe'en,' the creature replied. But it's February, so why is it here now!

Lydia Ramsden (11)
Lutley Primary School, Halesowen

Walking The Plank

Lying behind the barrels, I didn't breathe. The rickety boat was rocking, the drunken pirates were singing and I wasn't meant to be there. I moved precariously on the deck, reaching for some food. The box fell, the food streamed endlessly on the floor.
'Who goes there?' the captain screamed.

Jacob Upcott (11)
Lutley Primary School, Halesowen

The Weeping Terror

The angel stood in the garden, disguising his eyes, as if he were weeping. I blinked. The angel was in my face, his eyes bulging, no pupils, just the eye. He had no expression. His mouth like razors, ready to gobble up a … What was that? The angel had disappeared!

Amy Ryan (11)
Lutley Primary School, Halesowen

Picky Princess

She was bored. There was no other way of putting it. The princess was waiting for her prince charming and had been for three years. Suddenly there was a bang! A man popped up over the wall.

'Eww, you're ugly.'

She pushed him over and continued brushing her long hair.

Lauren Embrey (11)
Lutley Primary School, Halesowen

The Beast

There I was staring at it. It had got up. I ran for the door, it had disappeared. I ran for a window that had gone as well and then it pounced back at me, then everything was a blur.

Thomas Sprogis (11)
Mount Nod Primary School, Coventry

Sailing Disaster

I was sailing. Suddenly my heart was pounding and I couldn't breathe! I waited … Nobody was around to help! What could I do? Suddenly lightning flashed. My ship was sinking! I was unconscious! I fell into the water … The next thing my eyes opened. I was on shore!

Shannon Stevenson (11)
Mount Nod Primary School, Coventry

The Magic Dolphin

The waterfall's sparkling crystal-blue water fell as Sally was swimming. She loved the tranquillity and calmness. The water's current was too strong and took her down, Sally struggled! Something swam towards her bringing her to the surface. She woke up, dreaming about magic dolphins! Was it only a dream?

Connie Teggin (10)
Mount Nod Primary School, Coventry

The Bermuda Triangle

There was a faint mist rapidly appearing in the distance, she drifted westwards. Suddenly there was chaos and yelling. The figure was slowly disappearing. Everything was quiet, the mist had got thicker. Then it had gone. The sea was lonely, the Sun Princess had vanished.

Sarah Didcott (10)
Mount Nod Primary School, Coventry

Spice World

The Spice Girls are getting ready for their live show. Their names are Geri, Emma, Melanie C, Victoria and Melanie B. They also have group names that are Ginger, Baby, Sporty, Posh and Scary. They really enjoyed doing their live show. Their manager Clifford he was very proud.

Jeneitha-Ashley Walker (10)
St Bernadette's RC Primary School, Yardley

Mysterious Disappearance

Drip-drop went the basement tap. I told stories to myself about the disappearance of Miss Lakin. Her house was always dark so I went in. I found a machine. Time machine. Miss Lakin was trapped. Mr Kingston trapped her. '999, the police,' I said. Miss Lakin is free.

Laura Ryan (10)
St Bernadette's RC Primary School, Yardley

The Indignant Footballer

The coach was giving frantic gestures and signs posting madness around the pitch. The protesting went on until an indignant player whacked the ball on the head of their coach. 'You nasty little rat!' he yelled dreadfully in pain. The player was satisfied and went away giggling.

Cathareen Babu (10)
St Bernadette's RC Primary School, Yardley

The Deadly Hallway

I creep slowly through the hallway. *Creak,* go the old dusty wooden floorboards. I'm surrounded by cobwebs and mouse droppings, it isn't very pleasant. I keep going down this ghastly hallway. *'Argh!'* I scream. A man with a large axe comes running up to me! Then suddenly! I wake up!

Yanieke Neale Williams (10)
St Bernadette's RC Primary School, Yardley

The Horrid Thing

I was bobbing up and down. I was feeling dizzy and hot and then I stopped. I stood up and wobbled. I felt something coming up and it was getting closer. It then came up out of my mouth, sick, *sick.* I so wish I was not scared of boats.

Molly Nevin (10)
St Bernadette's RC Primary School, Yardley

The Alien

We cycled past Gorson Park. Suddenly a UFO fell near the middle of the park. As Adam and I cycled towards it we realised an alien was standing outside it! We tried to run but were too scared. We screamed, 'Help!' Men came running towards us and the alien fled.

Athif Hussain (9)
St Bernadette's RC Primary School, Yardley

Ghost

I was forced back against the door. I jumped quickly out of the way and ran down the gloomy, dark corridor and went into a room with many cupboards so I got in one. Then I felt something breathing down my neck. I turned, 'Mum that wasn't a nice trick!'

Daniel Tonks (10)
St Bernadette's RC Primary School, Yardley

The Shaun Of The Dead

Once before we were born zombies took over Earth. Then a boy was born but wasn't zombie. He grew up fast and killed a lot but there was a master zombie. He was very strong but the boy killed him and all of the rest of the zombies turned human.

Josh Walsh (10)
St Bernadette's RC Primary School, Yardley

The Stranger

Am I alone, really alone in the darkness of the night in a place I don't know. What's that breathing down my neck? I turn, startled by the heavy breathing. I run but there's no escape. I feel cold hands envelop me then what has happened? I am gone.

Joseph Ball (9)
St Bernadette's RC Primary School, Yardley

The Chase!

I was running faster and faster from this insane creature. Not daring to look back. I wondered how far away it was from me, but sadly I knew it wasn't far. I heard its footsteps tremble, I heard the roaring stop, then suddenly I knew, I was unharmed and … alive!

Brittany MacDonald (10)
St Bernadette's RC Primary School, Yardley

Rainbows

A multicoloured spaceship landed over Ireland. Five hours later Ireland became a rainbow. Its people, leprechauns and its pot of gold at the end of it.
Two days later rainbows were scattered over the world. That's how rainbows came about.

Alexandra Spence (9)
St Bernadette's RC Primary School, Yardley

The New House

The sale sign went up! Mom and Dad had to show the house to a lot of strangers. We packed the boxes. Finally the house was sold! The boxes were taken in a big removal van. When we arrived it felt strange at first, but it felt like home!

Bethany Smallwood (10)
St Bernadette's RC Primary School, Yardley

The Bermuda Triangle

Flying at 4,000ft, about to enter the Bermuda Triangle the whole plane begins to shake. I hold the seat, my hands turn white, sweat runs down my face. People scream, the windows break. A crew member gets hit by flying glass. The plane is going down. Suddenly … I wake up.

Adam Smiley (10)
St Bernadette's RC Primary School, Yardley

The Disastrous Journey

I knew that this was a terrible idea, first I felt really sick and went pale in the face, next we broke down because we had no petrol, so we had to push the car. What will be next? Well nothing! We were finally at our destination. At last!

Georgia McGuire (10)
St Bernadette's RC Primary School, Yardley

The Magic Show That Goes Wrong

The man walked on stage, he was doing a magic trick. He put a duck in a box. Then we found out he had two ducks. When he was pulling the cover from the other duck, the one in the box flew out. It was a big, big, big disaster.

Samantha Gartland (9)
St Bernadette's RC Primary School, Yardley

Merlin

Merlin was trying to make an age potion, he added the frog's eyes into the cauldron. *Bang! Pop! Fizz!* it went. Merlin was so shocked at that he knocked the cauldron over and fell in the potion. He grew older and older by the minute. Suddenly he exploded and disappeared.

Shannon Meakin (10)
St Bernadette's RC Primary School, Yardley

The Spaceship That Cleaned Birmingham

A cold windy day. Everyone in Birmingham stood still. Hovering in the sky a large strange UFO similar to a drink can made its way towards the ground, everything recyclable was drawn to it like a magnet. Within seconds Birmingham was clean. Now it is a city to be proud of.

Ashley Wear (10)
St Bernadette's RC Primary School, Yardley

What's Behind The Door?

I heard a noise … I silently went down to see what was happening, as I reached the door handle my hands started sweating, my throat went dry, it felt like I'd been strangled, my neck was twisted too. I opened the door, a man was hanging, it was Dad, *aarrgh!*

Aimee Rose (10)
St Bernadette's RC Primary School, Yardley

Nightmare

I hear a buzz and it travels through my ears into my whole body. My breathing becomes fast, my skin attracts my clothes. Pacing towards the door, I stop terrified and head to my closet. I hear footsteps, the door opens, I see black. I'm falling, but where? What's happened?

Phillippa Hunter (10)
St Bernadette's RC Primary School, Yardley

Losing My Grip

As my grip gradually loosened, so did my thoughts. Suddenly my tense focus to hold on faded abruptly and feelings from my sweaty palms and trembling heart were lost. I was safe now, I was free. Though my heart was in my mouth I was free and I was flying.

Abigail Hunter (10)
St Bernadette's RC Primary School, Yardley

The Angel!

I was walking one day, I heard something strange. It was unusual and not seen. The wind was blowing slowly and trees were moving. Something was there. It felt warm but I could not see. Was it a bird? Was it a leaf? I don't know. It's incredible, an angel!

Aimé Dickson (10)
St Bernadette's RC Primary School, Yardley

Lost

Matthew looked around but he couldn't see anyone. The house had turned into a winding tunnel, a labyrinth. Matthew ventured on. Slowly, slowly he turned a dark, damp corner. He heard a rustling. *Help!* A big dark form came towards him. It was only mum looking for her lost bunny.

Jamilah Mohammed (9)
St Catherine of Siena RC Primary School, Lee Bank

Triangle Of Death

Quiet. There was no noise but the sound of the shimmering water. Suddenly they entered the Bermuda Triangle. Slowly ... slowly sweat dripped down my body as waves began to crash over the wooden boat. The boat sank. All were dead. Dare you enter the Bermuda Triangle? I made a mistake.

Sineade Bates (10)
St Catherine of Siena RC Primary School, Lee Bank

Norbert And The Water Dragon

Norbert skipped to the ocean where a dragon 'apparently' lived. Suddenly a great wave of water appeared from behind the rocks, there was something there. It was huge! It was heavy and it was mighty! Two wings, an immense head emerged, it was a dragon. What should Norbert do? Run!

Natalie Maybury (11)
St Joseph's Catholic Primary School, Darlaston

Mysterious Car

Laura rushed out of school in the pouring rain. She ran across the road but tripped. Laura carefully examined her knee. At the same time a black car came down the road. She turned the corner and the car followed. The car door opened, it was her mum. New car!

Abigail Armstrong (10)
St Mary's RC Primary School, Wednesbury

Humpty Was Pushed!

Humpty was pushed on top of the king's horses and king's men. Suddenly he felt a hand and then a foot. Next thing he knew he was going down, down, down. The next day when people were going to work, they saw yolk all over the floor. What was it?

Paige Bullock (10)
St Mary's RC Primary School, Wednesbury

The Mysterious Car

Laura rushed out of school, through the gates and across the road. In her hurry, she tripped and fell! *Screech!* Laura looked up to see a black car! The door opened … Laura's heart thudded … from the car came one black boot, then a second … 'Oh, hello Mom,' Laura sighed deeply!

Paige Callear (11)
St Mary's RC Primary School, Wednesbury

Time Trouble

'Tick-Tock!' The clock chimed 9pm. Amy was late home again! She crept up the stairs. She hurried to the top to find her door open! Who was in there? She peered into her room tentatively. Suddenly a dark object jumped up. 'Aaargh! … Oh silly dog! Phew.'

Nicole Caulfield (11)
St Mary's RC Primary School, Wednesbury

The Voices

'Ouch!' someone screamed in pain.
'Help me,' the cries got louder and louder.
'Help,' was all she heard.
'Argh!' she had woken. Why had she been hearing these things? No she couldn't be? Was she? Well she wouldn't believe it at all!
'Help,' whispered voices. Where were they coming from?

Rachel Cutler (11)
St Mary's RC Primary School, Wednesbury

Magic Umbrella

Lucy got a new umbrella from her mom. Whenever she opened the umbrella it started to rain. She closed it. The rain stopped. 'How could this be?' Suddenly the umbrella flew away and Lucy could hear her mom's voice. 'Lucy get up the roof's leaking!' Lucy grabbed her umbrella.

Aliya De Vini (11)
St Mary's RC Primary School, Wednesbury

The Greedy Cat

Oh no, it's dinner time and where is Sam Cat, he needs to eat? His owner looks in the garden and in the house, he isn't there! His owner looks over the gate and there he is eating some treats and cat food from his next-door neighbour, Elly Tombs.

Chantelle Grove (11)
St Mary's RC Primary School, Wednesbury

The Hairy Hedgehog

Harry was a hairy hedgehog who had bristles like big branches. His quest was to cross the road to get to the pot of gold. Harry was amazed to find that the road was clear. Harry made a run for it moving his little legs as fast as lightning. *Crash ...*

Ryan Flowers (11)
St Mary's RC Primary School, Wednesbury

Monkey Madness

There once was a monkey who wanted a banana. He climbed up the mountain and ran past the mad monkeys. Finally he reached the banana and it swung out and attacked him. The monkey ran as fast as he could. Run, run, run. Now he's safe lying in his bed.

Megan McNally (11)
St Mary's RC Primary School, Wednesbury

Ria And The Loch Ness Monster

'Ria, don't go in the water,' shouted Nathen but Ria ignored him and went for a swim. Little did she know what was about to happen. As she dived in Nathen shouted, 'Look out! Loch Ness monster!' Ria swam quickly to shore as a black tyre bobbed up behind her!

Siobhan Wilkes (11)
St Mary's RC Primary School, Wednesbury

The Armies That Time Forgot

It was the day of war. The war that everyone would remember, the whole world united, forgetting all the old hatred. I was on the frontline as the armies of time chased. We stood firm. They hurled rocks from the darkness. Then fell reducing to dust and ashes an illusion.

Tomasz Zielinski (11)
St Mary's RC Primary School, Wednesbury

Shadow Monster

Dark, lonely creatures lurk amongst the narrow streets of London. Eyes red as fire in Hell and mouths full of teeth like a thousand blades. Fingers bony and long with deadly large talons curled around their body. Not touchable just visible. Everybody went down there but none came back!

Katie Ellis (11)
St Patrick's RC Primary School, Walsall

Bad Dream - Shadow Monster

A dark, lonely, mysterious creature lurked in the shadows of the alleys. Eyes as red as fire in Hell and teeth like thousands of daggers and blades sank into my skin. I screamed for help, but no sound came out.
'Denise, Denise, wake up!' Mum shouted. I sighed with relief.

Denise Pacurza (11)
St Patrick's RC Primary School, Walsall

Fairy Fantasy

I was sunbathing in my garden when suddenly I heard a fluttering in my ear. I jumped upright but nothing was there. I dashed to the bottom of the garden. Glitter fell upon my shoulders. A beautiful fairy dressed in yellow, tiny red shoes, golden hair said, 'Oh hello there.'

Charlotte Rich (10)
St Patrick's RC Primary School, Walsall

Oops!

Crash! Oops, I've done it again! *Bang! Bang! Bang!* Here comes the alien. The spaceship opens and a gruesome creature bawls at me, 'Come with me little girl! You're going to be grounded for a very long time!' and with that I'd lost my ball for four whole weeks!

Georgia Allen (10)
St Patrick's RC Primary School, Walsall

The House

One night my mate and I went to a deserted house. We opened the door and crept in. Suddenly there was a creak from upstairs. We tiptoed up. The bathroom door opened, it was my mom. She followed me into the house. She scared me.

Joseph McNally (10)
St Patrick's RC Primary School, Walsall

Wicked Women

Rosie was walking home from school. She got home to find her mom turning into an evil wicked witch called Mrs Richards. Then she saw her dad was turning into an alien. She shouted aloud, 'Help! Help!' She sprinted out of the house. She didn't know where to go.

Emily Mace (10)
St Patrick's RC Primary School, Walsall

The Deadly Forest

It was a dark night. The door creaked open. It slammed back shut. 'Is anybody there?' whispered the boy. He shook like the wind blowing some leaves.
Someone not far said quietly into his ear, 'You are dead.' That day reminded me of when I was dying in the forest.

Callum Wigley (10)
St Patrick's RC Primary School, Walsall

The Pile Of Clothes That Came To Life

Melanie was an untidy girl and after a while a pile of clothes, built up to the ceiling. One night while she was asleep the pile woke. It was huge, it was alive, it could eat Melanie. It tossed her in the air and gobbled her up in one bite!

Michaela Jenkins (10)
St Patrick's RC Primary School, Walsall

Dragon Alert!

It was Hallowe'en! Sam was going trick or treating. He dressed up as a devil. When he got there a dragon was opposite, 'Argh!' Sam ran.
Knock. 'Trick or treat?'
'One moment.'
'Oh thanks.' Sam ran and bumped into the dragon. He took off the face, it was just Josh.

Sophie Dabbs (10)
St Patrick's RC Primary School, Walsall

Pikachu's Vacation

One day Pikachu went into the haunted house and Totodile went in. 'Boo!' Haunter came and used Dream Eater and they carried on.
'Surprise!' everyone shouted.
It was their 400th anniversary they had a great time. 'Thanks guys, *sniff, sniff.*'
Everyone cried. They had cake. It was really great.

Melissa Powell (10)
St Patrick's RC Primary School, Walsall

The Beast

The beast awoke. He started to charge through the forest. *Slice!* The prince sliced off some of its hair. The beast began swiping at the prince who elegantly dodged the slashes.
'*Roar,*' growled the beast and he jumped at the prince. *Stab!* The beast died, the war was over finally.

Harry Smith (10)
St Patrick's RC Primary School, Walsall

The Dragon

The dragon I saw had bright green eyes. He had claws as sharp as knives and as white as bread. He was as long as a football pitch and his tongue was like a fork coming in and out of his mouth. His body was scaly … Then I woke up.

Caoimhe Harvey (10)
St Patrick's RC Primary School, Walsall

Aliens

Walking home one night I saw flashing lights in the sky. I wanted to investigate more so I went closer. I saw that it was a spaceship. I stepped on board and saw a green person. I thought it was an alien. I had discovered life from another planet.

Lucy Westwood (9)
St Patrick's RC Primary School, Walsall

The Party

The new girl was called Rose. She was the double of me! People got us mixed up. I went home and told my mom, she went as white as a ghost! I went to a party that night and found out she was my twin sister.

Bonnie Ryder (11)
St Patrick's RC Primary School, Walsall

FS (Friend Sisters)

There were two girls who were enemies, they never liked each other. But two years later, they became friends because they had to sit next to each other. Three years later they noticed that they behaved the same, so they called themselves FS (friend sisters) and they still are now.

Shannondeep Gill (11)
St Patrick's RC Primary School, Walsall

The Haunted Dance School

There was a dance school called Grange Manor, Belinda walked briskly to the door. One day she went upstairs to get some equipment. She turned around and a man was creeping closer. She was never seen again. From then on whenever someone went upstairs she waited then killed them …

Amber Wilson (10)
St Patrick's RC Primary School, Walsall

The House Of No Return

Elle's school day had finished. She took a shortcut through the woods past this strange house. She decided to go inside the house. Elle was in shock, next minute in the house no one was there. She was never seen again.

Leah Anslow (11)
St Patrick's RC Primary School, Walsall

The Hot Day

Martin stared blankly at his watch. The heat started to burn. He began to sweat as the sun beat down. Suddenly to his horror, his hand was melting! Then his arms, legs, feet. Soon there was no trace of where he had been …
Then he woke up.

Ryan Edge (10)
St Patrick's RC Primary School, Walsall

The New Girl

It was a day that a new girl arrived at our school but what was her name? I didn't know. The girl came in the classroom. She looked very shy, her name was Jade. She sat next to me. A week later in the class we had become best friends.

Lauren Aulton (10)
St Patrick's RC Primary School, Walsall

A Birthday Story

As I walked through the door it was silent. I had searched round the whole entire house but there was no one in. Surely somebody is home now. Mum and Dad shouted, 'Happy birthday Jim! I bet you thought we had forgot!'

Simran Singh Uppal (11)
St Patrick's RC Primary School, Walsall

Down The Drain

Down the drain lurks a monster you only dream about, but trust me, he's real. Its scaly body is slimy and gooey with eyes so red that when you look at them they burn you. He's lived down there for some time … you never know when he might come out!

Sian Gallagher (11)
St Patrick's RC Primary School, Walsall

FS2 The Surprise Party

Soon it would be Ellie's birthday so Libby decided to throw her a surprise party. Eventually Ellie's birthday came, Libby and all her friends couldn't wait. When Ellie got home everywhere was quiet. Then suddenly everyone jumped out at her and shouted, 'Surprise!' and that was Ellie's best birthday ever.

Zoë Langley (11)
St Patrick's RC Primary School, Walsall

Dream Or Not A Dream

My turn to perform! I thought, *one chance to impress the judges.* It was time to shine. Here we go! I was nervous, I ran on stage. No one was there! No judges! It's over, my dream wrecked. But something popped in my head! Was it a dream or not?

Clare Newton Sheppard (11)
St Patrick's RC Primary School, Walsall

The Celebrity Surprise Party

I was in my VIP limo driving to the MTV awards. When I got in there was nobody there so I turned around and everyone was waiting for me, yes! Celebrities were singing happy birthday to me. It was the best birthday ever!

Antoinette Chiwambo (11)
St Patrick's RC Primary School, Walsall

Dripping

As fresh blood was repeatedly dripping from the ceiling, blood was filling up the room. I knew it was far from over. The blood was warm, I gasped for air. When I was about to die, I saw my dead parents watching me. My fear of water made me shake.

Thomas Gilfoyle (10)
Shirestone CP School, Tile Cross

The Shadow Upstairs

The man heard creaking upstairs. He went into the kitchen to get a knife. He went upstairs. There wasn't anyone there but then he saw a shadow and the shadow crept behind him. It grabbed the knife and it is safe to say the man wasn't seen again.

Kimberley Parrish (11)
Shirestone CP School, Tile Cross

Scary Story

The night was dark and misty, nobody could see anything. All we could see were the street lights flickering. It was very unusual they never flickered. I walked outside the gate and realised that there were a pair of bloody hands behind me. I screamed as loud as I could.

Tori Lynch (11)
Shirestone CP School, Tile Cross

A Whole New World

It was the night before my 13th birthday. I know I shouldn't go back as it has been like I have appeared from the dead. All I remember was my disappearance from my holiday park. It was at that time I had gone.

Hayley Bickley (11)
Shirestone CP School, Tile Cross

The Mini Man In The Wardrobe

James was on his computer when he heard a bang coming from his wardrobe. He moved in to look. In there was a man, a wizard. 'Who are you?' James asked.

'I'm Dave,' he said watching a bear. 'Pass me the rope.' James gave it to him.

Jessica Aldridge (11)
Shirestone CP School, Tile Cross

The Phone

I heard a scream. I was trembling from head to toe. I looked around, no one was there. All I could see were numbers. I'll never get over my fear of talking on my phone.

Kimberly Wedderburn (10)
Shirestone CP School, Tile Cross

The Aliens

Action hits town when an emerald alien bombs the town with his special gun. Everyone is screaming with fear. Fear ran down my spine. Unexpectedly it was approaching me, the town was destroyed, every little bit. Suddenly ten emerald aliens appeared out of nowhere.

Lamariya Alexander (10)
Shirestone CP School, Tile Cross

Bad Friends

My nightmare had arrived but not like now. I dreamt it. I couldn't catch my breath, only to find out it was a practical joke. With friends like mine you don't need enemies.

Niall Rowe (11)
Shirestone CP School, Tile Cross

Nightmare

I sat up in the heartbreaking hospital bed. I had to speak this minute. My legs were no longer there. I felt worthless with a grey cloud above my head. I asked myself, *will I be here tomorrow to see my great-grandchildren?* I felt my life ending.

Nicole Yates (11)
Shirestone CP School, Tile Cross

Midnight Disappearance

At midnight I ran away leaving no trace. Walking the gloomy streets, I heard footsteps in the alley. A dark figure approached me. My hands trembling, my courage faded. Before I knew it, I was completely sealed inside a dark, cold, lonely cell.

Nicole Bell (10)
Shirestone CP School, Tile Cross

The Creepy Goblin

In a creepy village lived a goblin, every night he would go out and kill people. However one night he found a person called Stuart. The goblin was just about to stab him when Stuart shot him in the heart about thirty times. Just then another goblin appeared. *Oh no!*

Kieran Moogan (10)
Shirestone CP School, Tile Cross

Dinner With My Wife!

I was in a romantic hotel having dinner with my lovely wife. She had pork chops and I had nothing. I was gazing at her. Suddenly I put my hand in my pocket and pulled out a ring and said, 'Will you marry me?' with a big breath, 'Pretty please?'
'Yes.'

Guy Brayne (10)
Shirestone CP School, Tile Cross

The Ugly Troll!

In a village there was an ugly troll. Everyone was scared of him. But when he went to the shop an old lady came up to him. She wasn't scared she liked him because she was blind. They got married. The old woman was named Nikkita. They were in love.

Kirsty Prescott (10)
Shirestone CP School, Tile Cross

Revenge Of The Dead!

It was the night of Friday 13th. There was a freezing breeze. I walked through a graveyard. Jamie and Blake got scared and screamed like girls. Then a crew of ghosts came standing out of their tombstones. Suddenly I had to run, just then I fell down …

Nathan Davies (10)
Shirestone CP School, Tile Cross

Creepy

It was dark, I walked down the corridor. Then there was a bang! Doors were slamming, curtains shaking. Then a light flickered on and off, the floor was creaking. Then the lights came on, it was the kids messing about!

Corey Hodges (10)
Shirestone CP School, Tile Cross

The Party

When Rosie came from school she saw that her dad and mom were not there. But a door opened and her mom and dad were in the bedroom because it was her birthday. She had a great party but then she ran up to bed and had a lovely sleep.

Emily Williams (8)
Shirestone CP School, Tile Cross

Moving House

Moving house is annoying because of packing and unpacking. But then a week later we unpacked more then we saw a ghost stomping downstairs. We were scared. At night we were really scared because we didn't know what was going to happen. But in the morning it wasn't that scary!

Georgia Mahon (8)
Shirestone CP School, Tile Cross

The Little Girl

Yesterday I went on holiday with my mom and dad. We went to Greece it was spectacular. We are catching fish tomorrow. I'm going to the beach because I met my new friend named Cloe. She is wonderful. I'm going home. 'Cloe where you going?'
'I'm going home bye.'

Shannon Rainey (8)
Shirestone CP School, Tile Cross

Rose And Jack

Once upon a time there was a boy called Jack and a girl called Rose. Jack said, 'Let's go to the park.'
Rose said, 'Okay then let's go.' So off they went. When they got there they saw Shanne. Shanne's phone rang, it was Shanne's mom saying, 'Come home now.'

Chloe Short (8)
Shirestone CP School, Tile Cross

Doctor Who

Doctor and Martha and the TARDIS were travelling in time. The TARDIS was middle-size and blue. Captain Jack rushed onto the TARDIS. When they landed Captain Jack lay on the floor. Martha went back into the TARDIS and got a health kit. Captain Jack woke up.

George Facer (8)
Shirestone CP School, Tile Cross

The Boogeyman

One sinister night Jake fell down a hole called the bottomless pit, he fell and fell until a worm caught him and gave him a mask. Jake turned into someone called the Boogeyman.
He now eats worms 24/7 non-stop. 'I'm the Boogeyman and I'm coming to getcha!'

Reece Drakeley (9)
Shirestone CP School, Tile Cross

My Surprise

I woke up, there was a knock at the door, I went to the door, there was no one there. The phone rang, I answered, no one there. I started to sweat. Then I went to the back garden. Everyone said, 'Surprise!'

Chad Fennell (11)
Shirestone CP School, Tile Cross

Fear

My fear approached me. My hands were shivering. I felt as if I was being hit by a massive ice cube. I heard an echo of a sinister howling noise. I was crying as if being shot. I wish I didn't have a fear of the woods.

Connor Bryan (11)
Shirestone CP School, Tile Cross

The Day After My Birthday

I was shaking I was that happy my arms reached the top of the sky, but then I started to get terrified as a chill ran down my spine and I went upside down, I now absolutely despise roller coasters that go upside down.

Kelly Brayne (11)
Shirestone CP School, Tile Cross

He Is Coming

I heard footsteps coming behind me, I started to run, I ran into a deserted house but I heard him follow me. Then I knew I was trapped. To reassure myself I said if I'm still and quiet I will be fine … I heard a bang and he was there.

Zoe Fincher (11)
The Ridge Primary School, Wollaston

The Fight

My lip trembled as his finger slipped over the trigger, he couldn't do it, we were best friends … He pulled it … a giant ball of red paint came hurtling towards me, I ducked but it came too fast and hit me on the nose. It hurt, but paintballing was great.

Jenny Supple (11)
The Ridge Primary School, Wollaston

Naughty Ned

I slowly crept down the stairs past the kitchen, past the lounge and out into the cold, moist garden. I took on the challenge of calling his name, 'Ned!' He slipped from his hiding place, he moved forwards. We slowly stepped back into the house. I fed Ned, the cat!

Jay Hill (10)
The Ridge Primary School, Wollaston

Midnight Mission

I silently slipped out of my bedroom and sneaked along the corridor. I stole a glance at my watch. Midnight. The wooden stairs groaned as I made my way down them. I had reached the kitchen. I had done it! My hands shot out for the object - the cookie jar.

Edmund Roffe (11)
The Ridge Primary School, Wollaston

No Way Out

I came round the corner, the way was clear. No one was there. I walked into the courtyard. Suddenly the robot caught me unaware, I dropped my astro sword, the robot raised his plasma gun to kill me. 'Jack, tea!' called Mum. I turned off the PlayStation and went downstairs.

Thomas Mander (11)
The Ridge Primary School, Wollaston

A Lucky Miss

I had to, I just had to. It was as if my entire life had been leading up to this, I aimed the laser. Someone behind me shot and missed but hit the other opponent, I spun round and shot. I'd just completed the hardest game in the world.

Samuel Price (11)
The Ridge Primary School, Wollaston

The Van

I set off on my journey. I looked at the coin, I stepped up to the van, put the coin on the counter and a hand came out holding the most amazing ice cream I had ever seen. I took a lick, an amazing flavour burst into my waiting mouth.

James Pennington (11)
The Ridge Primary School, Wollaston

The Descent

All of the seatbelt signs flicked on and the clicking of buckles being fastened filled the cabin. The plane tipped and everyone lurched forward violently. It felt like my stomach was climbing up my throat. I clutched my brother's hand tightly and waited silently for darkness to engulf us all.

Joe Upton (11)
The Ridge Primary School, Wollaston

The Laser Quest

I was surrounded, there was no way out. I would be humiliated, everyone would know! Charlie, Barry, Josh and Jerry were watching me, ready to stop my escape. I made a dash for it. I fell to the ground. They had lasered me, and my chances of winning.

Lauren Simmonds (11)
The Ridge Primary School, Wollaston

Long Way Down

Jane climbed up the ladder dreading what was ahead. All she could see through the hole was darkness. She sat on the edge wondering where she would end up. Then, with a push, she slid down screaming. Then she crashed into the multicoloured balls. 'I hate slides!' she shouted.

Daniella Beach (11)
The Ridge Primary School, Wollaston

I'm Scared Of Spiders

It grabbed me. I was scared. I was shouting for help but nobody heard me. It let me go. I was running but it was coming closer and closer. I was running as fast as I could. It grabbed me again. I was really scared now. I hate spiders!

Lisa-Marie Powell (11)
The Ridge Primary School, Wollaston

Alone

Marc walked around the corner as he walked to the front door, he opened the door. 'I'm home Mom' nobody answered. A chill filled the air as Marc crept to the kitchen. He heard the floor creak. Marc was scared then a reassuring voice from behind spoke. 'Don't be scared.'

Kirsty Trevis (11)
The Ridge Primary School, Wollaston

The Dreaded Feeling

The dry pink lips were creeping closer every second. Nothing could stop the sloppy, sucking feeling. My heart was pounding and my tummy was turning. I could feel my toast coming back up. The skeleton-like hands were touching my face. Argh! My gran kissed me on the lips!

Emma Griffiths (11)
The Ridge Primary School, Wollaston

You Drive Me Potty Sis!

Someone was there, he just knew, but his legs were as stiff as ice, he couldn't move. Suddenly the door creaked open and Paul closed his eyes. A strange disfigured shadow appeared …
'Surprise!'
'I hate it when you scare me like that Charlie! I'll get my own back you know.'

Bethany Howell (11)
The Ridge Primary School, Wollaston

Spaghetti Attack

Today I'm going to Italy, when I get there I'm having spaghetti Bolognese. I'm here, the spaghetti's lovely.
(10 minutes later) the spaghetti is wrapping around my arms, help the mince is slurping me up, help, I'm getting eaten.
Phew! It's only World Explorer 3 on my PSP!

Josh Hill (10)
The Ridge Primary School, Wollaston

Danger

I ran down the road scared terribly about it, the dreaded lights, the huge metal rod being jammed into me, the deadly spray being squirted into my mouth. The wait, sitting on a chair with loudspeaker staring at you constantly, waiting for it to say, 'The dentist will see you!'

Jacob Humphries (11)
The Ridge Primary School, Wollaston

The Flight

Brad sat in the aeroplane fastened tight in his seat, his hands trembling, sweat dripping down his forehead, his legs shaking. Then all of a sudden everything fell silent as the plane started to travel down the long runway. Then take-off, and he felt the shaking of the plane.

Chelsea Heathcote (10)
The Ridge Primary School, Wollaston

Spain

I was on holiday in Spain. We were driving along the coast, when we stopped. We walked down onto a beach, the sand was like talcum powder beneath my feet. As I entered the sea, I slipped before a wave. I was dragged under. I swallowed some salt water, ugh!

Jake Shilvock (11)
The Ridge Primary School, Wollaston

The Party

It was my party and my favourite present was my DS. My sister kept wanting a go so I told her to shut up and go away but she didn't, so I pushed her into my mom's cake. I got told off and I got sent to my room.

Amy Checketts (11)
The Ridge Primary School, Wollaston

Late For School

One day Jenny got out of bed and realised that she was late for school. She put on her clothes, ran downstairs and the clock said it was 5am. When she woke up again she actually was late for school. *Oops!*

Jasdeep Kang (10)
The Ridge Primary School, Wollaston

The Ear-Piercing Sound

The noise was ear-piercing. It was screeching through my ears. I dropped onto my knees. I couldn't bear it anymore, I ran out the room. Minutes later I went back in the room. I couldn't hear anything. The radio was off.

Alicia Hewins (11)
The Ridge Primary School, Wollaston

Aeroplane

As I swooped in the air, my face was dripping with sweat as we were going up and up. I held onto my mom's hand really tight. My ears went ever so bubbly so my mom gave me a sweet to help. I wish I wasn't scared of flying.

Leah Rudd (9)
Walmley Junior School, Walmley

Ann The Mermaid

There once was a beautiful mermaid who was very poor. Her name was Ann and one day she was swimming when she saw a piece of gold and another and another. Soon she found so much she quickly became the richest girl in the sea and is now very kind.

Beth Crawford (9)
Walmley Junior School, Walmley

The Spooky Shadow

The mansion was dark and spooky. I went inside, the door shut behind, a shadow was following me. I went to my room, my mother's book was flicking pages. The pencil was writing. 'Boo!' said a voice behind me. I nearly fell out of my skin. 'Boo!' it said again.

Jack Richards (8)
Walmley Junior School, Walmley

Deep, Dark Angry Forest

I was in the dark, deep forest and nobody could hear me. There were birds pecking out my eyes and lions were roaring and biting me. But the worst thing was I was never to be seen again in the deep, dark forest.

Mandip Jhitta (8)
Walmley Junior School, Walmley

The Little Mouse

As the animal scurried across the floorboards the cat miaowed. It woke nearly everybody up. The lights were put on to see what it was. Then they knew what it was and went to bed. Oh! I wish cats liked mice and I wish mice liked cats.

Amelia Bow (8)
Walmley Junior School, Walmley

The Hippo That Escaped

There was once a hippo speaking to a monkey. The monkey said to the hippo, 'I wish I could escape from these bars!'
'I wish I could too,' said the hippo.
One night the hippo smashed the bars open and they went into the street. 'At last we are free.'

Charlie Hale (8)
Walmley Junior School, Walmley

The Thing

I went to the creaky abandoned mansion, then I walked through the corridor and wandered about until I realised I was lost. I found a fire exit but part of the roof fell down and blocked my escape. Then a sudden shiver grabbed my spine and then it came …

Samuel Jones (9)
Walmley Junior School, Walmley

The Spooky Sleepover

We were talking when suddenly the door of the bedroom slammed. Everybody jumped, I was wondering what had happened when I saw a spider run across the floor. I rushed into my mom's bedroom, when I saw an even bigger spider. After that it was never the same ever again.

Georgia Fielding (9)
Walmley Junior School, Walmley

Sue's Walk

A girl called Sue went for a walk and a man came the other way. He lunged at her. Sue thought he was going to steal her purse. Sue grabbed her umbrella and started to whack him. The man fell to the ground. Poor guy! He had tripped over the kerb.

Lindsay Ewer (7)
Walmley Junior School, Walmley

The Missing Unicorn

Once there were two unicorns. They lived in a house in Norway. One was the mum and the other was a baby. One day they went for a walk. When the baby went north, the mum went east. The baby was lost. He told someone and his mother was found.

Kayleigh Sheward (9)
Walmley Junior School, Walmley

Beneath The Sea

The water was cool and sparkly. It was as sparkly as the sun. Shaun the Shark was swimming sharply as well as looking for fish. At last he found his prey and with his sharp teeth he dug into his prey.

Charlie Fellows (7)
Walmley Junior School, Walmley

Tigers

The sun was sparkling, the sky was blue. Terunce the Tiger was having a sunbathe. A young man sat in a truck nearby, Terunce smelt some steak, the man held a stick out with a piece of meat from the zoo. People were looking, the other tigers came to play.

Phoebe McHale (8)
Walmley Junior School, Walmley

The Hurricane Of Death And Destruction

The wind blew rapidly as the swirling vortex came closer and closer. People ran to shelters. Soon after, the hurricane had gone. No life survived. What would become of this land?

Scarlett Byfield-Levell (10)
Walmley Junior School, Walmley

The Jungle Lake

I was swimming in the jungle lake, swimming, swimming, swimming, then I saw something move in the water. I realised it was a big fat fish! It came swimming towards me getting closer, closer, closer. Then suddenly I woke up. I was sitting in the back of the yellow sub.

Joe Willetts (8)
Walmley Junior School, Walmley

Sheer Fright!

A feint figure flew across my face. I felt all cold and shivery and a silvery shadow jumped forward. So did my stomach. The booming voices of a hundred banshees echoed through my ears. I burst out through massive wooden doors. Oh how I hate being on a rollerghoster!

Vincent Peters (8)
Walmley Junior School, Walmley

Home Sweet Home

The door was open, I walked inside. There were two rooms. The first one was very small and walls were lined with armour. The second room, massive with 50 big tables and witches, 'Run, argh!'
'Hee.' It was a haunted castle. I ran back home. It was a dream.

Tommy Roberts (7)
Walmley Junior School, Walmley

The Sand Maze

Once upon a time in Florida someone was making a maze in the sand. This maze nearly filled the whole entire beach. A few days later someone came and tried it out. When she started she got on well at first but then she got lots of dead ends.

Grace Chaundy (8)
Walmley Junior School, Walmley

Horrid Henry's Bedtime

'Is he in bed?' asked Mum.
'Yes, and he was in bed for eight o'clock.'
'That's unusual' said Mum. His parents stood outside the room peeking in. Henry slipped downstairs and hid under the settee.
'Let's go and look for him,' Dad said crossly.

Mathew Williams (8)
Walmley Junior School, Walmley

Untitled

Once upon a time there was a prince who had a sharp sword. There was a dragon in the city destroying the buildings. The police went to kill the dragon. The dragon went to its lair, then came back speeding out. The prince held out his sword, 'Hooray!' everyone shouted.

Alex Nevin
Walmley Junior School, Walmley

The Noise

Once upon a time I was standing in the middle of my room at twelve o'clock midnight. There was a noise outside of my room. It went silent for a minute. But it burst in. It was my mom.

Alex Reely (8)
Walmley Junior School, Walmley

The Beach Maze

Once upon a time there was a little girl called Dannielle who was stuck on a beach in a maze and couldn't get out with people seeing her because she was famous. One day she finally got out and said, 'Oh I'm exhausted and I need a drink.' And went.

Olivia Austin (7)
Walmley Junior School, Walmley

The Lonely Lion

There was once a lonely lion in a forest. It went past a lonely princess. The princess said, 'Why are you so grumpy?'
'Because I've got nobody to play with.'
'Can I play with you?'
'Yes of course you can, come on let's skip through the woods together.'
'Let's go.'

Hannah Peters (8)
Walmley Junior School, Walmley

Charlotte's Web

There once was a spider called Charlotte. She was a pretty spider. She made webs with words on them. She had a friend called Wilbur and he was a lovely pig. She was a really kind spider and always looked after people and animals. She never was mean.

Sophie Haynes (8)
Walmley Junior School, Walmley

The Princess

Once upon a time there was a princess who wasn't treated like one. She heard her sisters chatting about a ball where the prince would be. Suddenly a fairy godmother came and let the princess go to the ball. She had met the prince and danced all night long. The end.

Kyra Nagra (8)
Walmley Junior School, Walmley

The Alien

It was a dark night. Wolves were howling. No birds were singing. It was so dark. I heard a voice then an alien came in. I think its name was Zog. It turned its back. I woke up. I wish I never dream again.

Matthew Calvin (8)
Walmley Junior School, Walmley

The Lonely Child

There once was a lonely child, it was a girl called Monika, she lived in a palace. One day she went out to the woods. Suddenly she saw a child so she said, 'Do you want to play with me?'

'Of course.' So they played all day long.

Ashley Ward (8)
Walmley Junior School, Walmley

The Fairy

Once upon a time there lived a pretty fairy. She lived upon a seabed. She had a friend. The boy had a furry coat and shiny blue eyes and he rode on a horse. They both went on the horse and rode far, far away and lived together.

Natasha Davis (8)
Walmley Junior School, Walmley

The Little Baby Orphan

Once there was a little baby on the street, she had been thrown out of her home. There was a little girl walking past, her name was Rebecca. So Rebecca picked the baby up and went to the owner and said, 'Shall I keep this baby?' And she said, 'Yes!'

Rebecca Turner (7)
Walmley Junior School, Walmley

The Magic Goal!

I smacked the ball, it was going right out of play but suddenly it swooped right back into play. Goal! I had scored. The crowd went wild. I had scored my first goal for Hevans Heros and in the last minute of the CB Cup. Yippie!

Oliver Perrins (9)
Walmley Junior School, Walmley

The Fright Of Your Life

'Argh! It's really fast!' cried Sophie as she was on the supersonic rollercoaster at Drayton Manor Park. It was called 'Fright of your Life'. It was all part of her best friend's birthday party. 'That was great,' lied Sophie. It really was the fright of her life.

Lauren Harris (9)
Walmley Junior School, Walmley

Untitled

Finlay screamed at the top of his voice. His stomach suddenly jumped forward. He felt like he was going to be sick. He felt as if he was jumping out of an aeroplane, it was so painful he almost cried. If only he wasn't scared of lifts.

George Evans (9)
Walmley Junior School, Walmley

Jamie's Fangs

Jamie the vampire awoke one morning and went to the window, where he usually put his fangs before bedtime, but today they weren't there. He went downstairs and eventually ate his breakfast. He looked all over for them but couldn't find them. But when he scratched his head, 'Ouch!'

Michael Hartigan (9)
Walmley Junior School, Walmley

Mad Magic

Charlotte Mainsly thought she was the best at everything and outshined everybody at Major Magic School. One day Charlotte went to disappearing class. She picked up her wand and said a spell, *oops,* she had pointed the wand at herself! Good job she wasn't a real witch, thank God!

Remmi Kennedy (9)
Walmley Junior School, Walmley

A Surprise Birthday

Rosie had just arrived home from Sophie's house. She had been to see Sophie's new puppy called Tilly. When they came in she couldn't see anyone. When she was going upstairs to show Sophie something, 'Surprise!' 'Wow! Mum and Dad this is the best party ever. Have a drink please.'

Hannah Walker (9)
Walmley Junior School, Walmley

The Dream

The wind was howling and the vortex was coming closer and closer. I tried to steer my tiny, battered blue rowing boat away from the swirling whirlpool when suddenly … I woke up screaming. *'Aagghh!'* I yelled. Oh how I hate bad dreams.

Catherine Read (10)
Walmley Junior School, Walmley

Help Me

I was shaking. My teeth were chattering. I was upside down. I was so scared I jumped. I thought I was on a ride. Then my sweets went flying in the air. Then someone tapped me awake. It was my mum saying, 'Are you all right?'
It was a dream!

Claire Matthews (9)
Walmley Junior School, Walmley

Best Friend's Club

Rachel got sent home in disgrace from her school. Her mum and dad were going to move Rachel to another school. So they did. Rachel met Bethan and Jake. They asked Rachel if she would play with them. 'Yes!' she said. For the first time she had best friends.

Lauren Cox (9)
Walmley Junior School, Walmley

The Worst Ever Journey

My stomach turned over as we whizzed along and kept turning till we slowed down a bit. I saw a huge figure zoom past. Suddenly I was sick all over the floor. The high breeze made my hair blow all over the place. I hate going on the motorway.

Nickie Morris (8)
Walmley Junior School, Walmley

Nightmares

Which door? I was lost! The round, square, triangle or a keyhole one. I heard noises. I sneaked through the triangular door. Oh no, what a big mistake … *'Aarrgh!'*
'Looks like someone had fun in their dreams.'
'You wouldn't like it Mum so stop laughing!'
'Chill, it was a nightmare!'

Priya Sandhu (9)
Walmley Junior School, Walmley

A Spell That Went Wrong

He fired the spell but little did Daniel know that his wand was the wrong way round, it backfired and Daniel suddenly started belching up slugs! They quickly hurried to Albert's house where Albert gave Daniel a bucket.
One week later he was running around with his friends again.

Georgia Archer (9)
Walmley Junior School, Walmley

The Spooky Boat

The boat was dark and spooky, a pirate was walking up to Tim. He is my friend. Slowly and steadily Tim was walking back. *Aarrrgghh!* I heard. I tiptoed away to the door. Soon I was shaking so quick. I knew never ever to go on a pirate boat again.

David Fentham (9)
Walmley Junior School, Walmley

The Scariest Night Of My Life

The hall was darkened as Penelope walked through the house. There was a loud noise which sounded like cats screaming. The more she walked, the louder it got. Then boom! All of a sudden lights started flickering then a cold hand grabbed her! 'Boo! I've been trying to scare you!'

Kellie Brooke (9)
Walmley Junior School, Walmley

The Big Roar

There was an alarming noise outside. It felt like an earthquake, I thought the house was going to fall down. Me and my family huddled together in fear. After ten minutes the roar died. I'm so glad the house didn't fall down. I realised it was a car engine.

Arun Kalwan (11)
Yew Tree Primary School, Walsall

The Bomb

He looked up, the timer on the bomb counted down. Ruben, a capable boy, tried to stop the bomb exploding. Despite the fact that he was terrified, he tried to stop the bomb. The timer on the bomb was 0:10 seconds. Without thinking he cut a wire. The bomb stopped silently.

Dale Groves (11)
Yew Tree Primary School, Walsall

Walking On Death Row

As the bullets (each with the words deathrow marked on the side) left the gun, Andrew jumped onto the first bullet and walked over them. When he got to the end he drew his sword and sliced his enemy in half.

David Robinson (10)
Yew Tree Primary School, Walsall

Military Attack

Suddenly, the bomb exploded, tanks rushed out, it ended up being a military attack. The terrorists were on the run, military members could see the escape helicopter. The military launched missiles. Terrorists could run no more so they stopped running.

Tamjid Ahmed (10)
Yew Tree Primary School, Walsall

The Dream

'Don't eat me …' shouted Rupert concealed behind a saturated bushy thorn bush. The hippogrift he was observing outstretched his wings and flew out of sight. 'Get up Rupert Rickman's goin' to hit you,' Emma shouted. Rupert sat up to find Rickman hit him. 'Yey potions,' shouted Rupert …

Ashley Durnall (11)
Yew Tree Primary School, Walsall

Fast And Furious Tokyo Drift

There was a loud noise outside. It was like the world had fallen down. However, it was a car engine. The car was going to race a Subaru. The Subaru was very slow. The Evo is very fast, but it has got 1,000 brake horse power.

Ryan Hollingworth (11)
Yew Tree Primary School, Walsall

Untitled

One day Joe saw a house that had been abandoned. So he went in. He heard a creak but he did not make it. He went into the dull, forbidden room, with gruesome food on the table. 'Argh …' He was never seen again.

Jordan Spittle (11)
Yew Tree Primary School, Walsall

Untitled

Hurriedly, Emily observed the clean, shimmering house. The walls were made of shining gold and the floor was made of vibrant marble. Everything was as neat as a pin. However, next door was a scruffy, dull junkyard. Emily ambled into the clean house and there was a thief. Emily fainted.

Gabriella Orthodoxou (11)
Yew Tree Primary School, Walsall

The Atomic Bomb

He saw the bomb. He had just 50 seconds to stop the bomb. He got a cold wet cloth and put it over the bomb. It stopped straight away. He saved the world, his mom was so pleased, my hero.

Danny Hill (11)
Yew Tree Primary School, Walsall

Hallowe'en Horror

It was a terrifying sight. I had vampires coming at me from one side. There were zombies on the other side. There were witches in front of me. There were ghosts behind me. I had to admit, the costumes were good, but I could tell that they were my friends.

Calum Richardson (11)
Yew Tree Primary School, Walsall

Cinderella

There once was a girl and she had two very annoying and very ugly sisters. Cinderella - a very energetic person - always wanted to go to a ball with a handsome young man, and one day she did and it was a tremendous ball because then she lived happily ever after.

Emma Carter (11)
Yew Tree Primary School, Walsall

Untitled

Cinderella worked day and night to make her evil stepsisters dresses for the prince's ball. When everyone had gone to the ball Cinderella was working. Then *poof* her fairy godmother appeared and got her ready for the ball and took her. She danced all night. Her dream came true.

Aleisha Lawley (11)
Yew Tree Primary School, Walsall

Taking The Building

The squad moved closer to the building. They went in, up then to the window. They saw the enemy. There was a bang! They thought it was over but then they realised it was just an exercise for the US Special Forces Squad.

Callum Whitehouse (11)
Yew Tree Primary School, Walsall

Information

We hope you have enjoyed reading this book - and that you will continue to enjoy it in the coming years.
If you like reading and writing, drop us a line or give us a call and we'll send you a free information pack.
Alternatively visit our website at www.youngwriters.co.uk

Write to:
Young Writers Information,
Remus House,
Coltsfoot Drive,
Peterborough,
PE2 9JX
Tel: (01733) 890066
Email: youngwriters@forwardpress.co.uk